THE FARM
COMBINE

INVENTIONS THAT CHANGED OUR LIVES

THE FARM COMBINE

Ross R. Olney

WALKER AND COMPANY New York

ACKNOWLEDGEMENTS

The author would like to thank the following for photos, advice, and technical information: Gregory Lennes and Jim Woodard from International Harvester; Gerald L. Purser from Allis Chalmers; and, especially, Will McCracken from John Deere, who has been more than generous with his time and knowledge in helping to get this book just right.

Library of Congress Cataloging in Publication Data

Olney, Ross Robert, 1929–
   The farm combine.

   (Inventions that changed our lives)
   Includes index.
   Summary: Traces the history of farm machines that combine the cutting and threshing processes and explains the importance of this invention enabling a single farmer to produce enough food for nearly fifty families.
   1. Combines (Agricultural machinery)—History—Juvenile literature. 2. Combines (Agricultural machinery)—Juvenile literature. [1. Combines (Agricultural machinery) 2. Agricultural machinery. 3. Farms. 4. Inventions] I. Title. II. Series.
S699.O46   1984   681′.7631   84-5288
ISBN 0-8027-6542-4

First published in the United States of American in 1984 by the Walker Publishing Company, Inc.

Published simultaneously in Canada by John Wiley & Sons Canada, Limited, Rexdale, Ontario.

Book designed by Lena Fong Hor

Printed in the United States of America
10 9 8 7 6 5 4 3 2 1

CONTENTS

PREFACE

CAN YOU NAME the three most important things in our lives?

They don't include money, or cars, or fancy jewelry. Not even a family, a good job, or a special hobby, although these are very important.

The three most important necessities in our lives are *food, clothing, and shelter.* And of these, *food* comes first. We cannot live without food. It is the fuel that makes our bodies run. Without it, we would starve.

Of all the food in the world, seeds and grain are the most important. If all seeds and all grain were to disappear from the face of the earth for one year, human life and most animal life would die off. After only one year, there would be nobody left.

For that reason, farmers are essential, and farm

equipment is vital to help them harvest seeds and grain.

There was a time when farmers had to cut grain with sickles, by hand. If the fields were large, some of the grain would rot before it could be cut. Most farmers, however, had small fields in earlier days.

Because farmers had smaller fields and used only hand equipment, their yields were small. In 1776, at the time of the American Revolution, the work of *thirteen* farmers was required to feed *one* person living in a city. Today, *one* farmer can produce enough food for his own family and *forty-six* other families.

Obviously, farmers have learned to grow crops better, and science has helped to improve farming methods. Seeds are better than they used to be, too. But there is one overriding reason why farmers are able to produce more food, and that is because of the invention and perfection of the *farm combine*.

1

Farming, An Ancient Occupation

SEEDS AND GRAIN have been on earth since before recorded history. They came from wild plants, and were even developed from weeds that couldn't be eaten. Man started to improve and cultivate grain for food as early as 5000 B.C. in Asia and Asia Minor. Farming methods began to be *scientific* as early as 4000 B.C. in Egypt, where the first "custom cutters" were farm workers who followed the harvest just as they do today.

These grain cutters, or reapers, were important people—so important that they were exempt from military service. To cut the grain, they used curved sickles. Some ancient sickles have been found in tombs. Of

In the days before machinery, farmers worked their fields by hand, using a sickle to cut the grain. *(John Deere photo)*

Another view of farm workers cutting grain by hand. *(John Deere photo)*

course, it took a great deal of muscle to reap and thresh grain in those days. A modern scientist recently took one of the old sickles and tried reaping some "einkorn" (an ancient wild cereal) in Turkey. He managed to harvest six-and-a-quarter pounds in one hour. This yielded two pounds of high-protein grain after threshing.

Man needed more than flint blades set into wooden or clay handles to cut grain and meet the growing demand.

Grain must be reaped and then threshed to be of any good to man. Reaping is cutting the grain. Threshing is removing the grain from its husk or ear. Both of these operations required a great deal of time. A skilled reaper, working with a hand sickle, could cut about one acre of wheat in a day.

Many inventors tried to develop new equipment to speed up the job, but, as simple as cutting crops might seem, it was very difficult to mechanize the job. Most of the would-be inventors failed, and sickles remained the popular tool for reaping. In ancient Turkey bronze sickles were even used as *money*. A man who owned many bronze sickles was a rich man.

Roman soliders carried the skills of ironworking to every corner of the known world. Far to the east, the Chinese were learning to harvest rice with sickles and threshing techniques. Still, much from these early-day crops was lost because farmers couldn't cut them quickly enough. When a crop was ready for reaping, the *whole* crop was ready.

Many people thought of different ways to mechanize harvesting. The Gauls, for example, who were great artisans and craftsmen, were among the first people to develop a machine to reap grain. The Roman historian and farmer, Pliny, described their machine: "On the vast estates in the provinces of Gaul, large frames fitted with teeth at the edge and carried on two wheels are driven through the corn by a pack animal pushing from behind. The ears thus torn off fall into the frame."

From this cart with teeth in front came the modern giants of today that thunder through vast fields of corn or wheat.

Reverend Patrick Bell was a Scot who worked his way through college and then divinity school. He was

always more interested in religion than in science and farming, but he did invent the first practical modern reaper. In fact, he was still a student at age twenty-five in 1826 when he noticed a pair of gardener's shears poking out of a hedge. It was all the inspiration the young Scot needed. He grabbed the shears, got down on his knees, and began to mow his way through some green oats in a nearby field.

"It was well no neighboring gossip saw me," Bell wrote later, "else the rumor might have been easily circulated that the poor student had gone crazed."

Bell persisted with his idea for a reaping machine, and in 1827 he built a model and then a full-sized wooden mockup. He hired a blacksmith to make the blades, but he wasn't satisfied with them, and finally he finished the cutting shears himself by hand. Even then, he noted, they gave him "a world of trouble and vexation. When they came into my hand they were in a very rude state and required my grinding, filing and fitting."

Bell's machine was loosely based on reapers built by inventors such as William Pitt, James Dobbs, French and Hawkins, James Ten Eyck, Robert Meares, Jeremiah Bailey, Joseph Mann, Robert Salmon, John Common, James Smith, Henry Ogle and

A farm tool, called a "cradle," was introduced to America in about 1776. It became the most effective way to cut grain. With a firm swing from right to left, the farmer could cut and throw the grain into a row, ready to be raked into sheaves. Using this tool, a worker could cut up to two acres per day per man. *(International Harvester photos)*

others. Each reaper would cut the grain by blades or cutters or a sawing motion, but none would do it really well. Building a reaping machine was *very* important. It was just that nobody could get it exactly right.

Nor did Reverend Bell, but his reaper seemed to work better than most. The trouble was, the straw was left scattered. It was, in Bell's own words, "lying higgeldy-piggeldy, in such a mess as would have utterly disgraced me in the harvest field."

Bell continued to work on his mechanism and by 1832 there were ten Bell reapers at work in Scotland.

A photo made from one half of an antique stereopticon slide of Hiram Moore's original combine at work between 1845 and 1850, the only photo available of this machine. *(John Deere photo)*

Each could cut ten acres a day and the cutters required sharpening after about fifty acres. Bell then turned full time to the ministry. He didn't even patent his designs. He believed the world of agriculture needed them more than he needed them. Bell died in 1869. His first reaper is in the London Science Museum today.

Still, before 1851, few farmers had ever set eyes on a reaper. It took American genius to invent and build the first truly efficient reaper, to revolutionize the harvesting task.

16

2

The McCormick Reaper

CYRUS AND ROBERT MCCORMICK, son and father, were also best friends and business partners. The two had worked together in the blacksmith's bellows business since Cyrus was a young boy. Cyrus was the oldest of three sons. The year he was born, 1809, his father had started working on a reaping machine. Robert McCormick knew of the work that had been done in Europe, and of the great need for a mechanized grain cutter. He was *certain* he had the answer.

The trouble was, Robert McCormick's reaper did not do what he wanted it to, no matter how hard he worked on it. He finally began to think it was an im-

Cyrus Hall McCormick, the inventor of the first modern reaper and a man who revolutionized the farm equipment industry. *(courtesy International Harvester)*

possible job. This was especially true on a day in 1816 when he demonstrated the reaper he thought would really work. And it didn't work.

Everyone laughed at McCormick and told him to stick with a business he knew. It wasn't that the McCormick family needed the money from a successful reaper. The family bellows business was doing just fine. They didn't really need to invent and sell reapers, but Robert McCormick was *certain* he could take the crude machines then available and build a real reaper. He knew he could make a reaper that would *work* over a period of time, that would cut grain mechanically and get it ready for threshing. But it was not to be.

Robert McCormick gave up on the reaper in 1831. So the son took over where the father left off.

Cyrus McCormick's first reaper was a crude machine. It stood on two wheels. The main wheel had attached to it the gearing that operated the cutting bars. The reaper was made of cast iron and both wheels had iron "tread" to keep them from slipping in the field.

The part of the reaper that did the cutting of the grain had a flat plate six feet long called the "cutting bar." Long steel points, called "guards," were riveted to this bar. The cutting was done by knives shaped like triangles attached to a steel bar that slid forward and backward in a groove in the guards. The knives moved

This is a painting of the great day in July 1831, when Cyrus McCormick first introduced his reaper to the public. *(courtesy International Harvester)*

A Marsh Harvester in a wheat field around 1875. Two men rode on the platform, binding grain by hand as it was cut. Earlier reapers required a crew of 4 or 5 men to do the binding. *(International Harvester photo)*

rapidly in the guards because of a gearing attached to the main wheel.

A divider separated the grain that was to be cut from the grain left standing. A reel bent the grain back against the knives and picked up the stalks that were lying close to the ground. This assured that all the grain was cut. As the grain was cut, it fell on a platform. A man walking along behind raked the grain off into piles; then it was collected and taken to the threshing floor.

The McCormick reaper and twine binder in 1881 was the first binder which tied the bundles with twine. This was a marvelous machine for its day, saving farmers a tremendous amount of work and thus allowing the opening of land for farming. *(International Harvester photo)*

This basic machine revolutionized grain-growing in the United States, making it possible to cut large fields of grain far more quickly. But Cyrus McCormick was critical of his machine. He even considered his father's advice to give up the dream of a reaper and devote attention to "more productive matters." But he didn't *take* the advice. Instead, he began to improve the reaper.

It was a good thing, too. Several inventors and farmers were working on reaping machines, and some

21

of them actually could cut some grain. McCormick had one chief competitor, a one-eyed, one-armed inventor by the name of Obed Hussey. Hussey was a seaman turned landlubber who invented a reaper similar to McCormick's. Unlike the other machines, which required the help of several farmers to run, both McCormick's and Hussey's reapers required only two-man crews.

Soon McCormick and Hussey were fighting in the press and on the field, each trying to prove that his reaper was better. Although Hussey's machines were good, McCormick's reapers won almost every competition and consistently outsold Hussey's machines among farmers.

Oddly, in those days *anybody* could get a patent. It didn't matter if somebody else had already invented nearly the same thing. You could even *copy* something that someone else had invented; and get a patent on it yourself. You got a patent certificate if you merely brought in plans. So both McCormick and Hussey had patents for reapers similar in design.

On his machine, Cyrus McCormick had notched out the smooth cutting blade to improve the cutting action. He made it more like some of the knives we have in our kitchens today with "serrated" blades for better cutting. McCormick labored over the parts of his machine to make it better and better. In 1839 he began to sell his model. By 1842, with a modified cutter bar that he positively guaranteed, he had sold seven units.

In his advertisements McCormick wrote that "purchasers would run no risk since, if the reapers for 1842 were not strong and endurable, and would not cut fifteen acres a day and save one bushel per acre, ordinarily lost by shelling when the cradle was used, they could be returned."

It was the first money-back guarantee in the farm equipment business, but there was trouble on the horizon. Obed Hussey thought his machines were better, and he was angered by the publicity McCormick was getting for his reapers. McCormick, in turn, was bothered every time one of Hussey's machines was mentioned by the press. Each inventor thought his machine was better. So began the "great American reaper war," in which the two inventors sniped at each other in newspapers through letters to editors.

McCormick wrote in *Mechanic's Magazine:* "I would ask the favor of you to inform Mr. Hussey and the public, through your columns, that the principle, viz. cutting grain by means of a toothed instrument, receiving a rotary motion from a crank, with iron teeth projecting before the edge of the cutter for the purpose of preventing the grain from partaking of its motion, is a part of the principle of my machine and was invented by me, and was operated on wheat and oats in 1831. I would warn all persons against the use of the aforesaid principle . . . as an infringement of my right."

Like a gunslinger from the Old West, Hussey rose to the challenge. He fired back: "Among those [attempts to produce a workable reaper] I consider myself alone successful. Every previous attempt has failed and gone into oblivion. My next year's machine will be much superior to any which I have before made and to which I apprehend but little improvement can subsequently be added."

McCormick's reaper was covered in an article in *The Southern Planter,* so Hussey took out pen and paper again—this time with a challenge. "I see from your *Planter* an account of another reaper in your State which is attracting some attention. It shall be my endeavour to meet this machine in the field in the next harvest."

The guns had been drawn. McCormick quickly accepted the challenge and the contest was held on a bright, sunny day in 1843 in Richmond, Virginia. Each machine cut a section of wheat. They even used the same team of horses so everything would be equal. Both reapers did well, but in a decision that left Hussey stunned, the judges chose *McCormick's* machine as best.

For the next several years Hussey kept writing against McCormick in the pages of magazines. Both men were selling their reapers. Finally, the editors called a halt to the matter.

Meanwhile, McCormick had been refining his machine even more. He added a self-raking device that would sweep the grain off into piles. Farm workers could pick it up for later threshing. This eliminated one man from the two-man crew needed to run the reaper. From then on it required only one farmer to drive the team of horses. By 1849, McCormick's improvements had moved the farmer off the back of a horse and onto the reaper itself.

In an action that stunned the farm equipment industry, McCormick introduced *credit* sales along with an ambitious advertising program. And his ads were straightforward.

I WARRANT MY REAPERS SUPERIOR TO HUSSEY'S AND ALL OTHERS. I HAVE A REPUTATION TO MAINTAIN. LET A FARMER TAKE BOTH AND KEEP THE ONE WHICH HE LIKES BEST, said one of McCormick's ads.

Although McCormick and Hussey and some others competed for years, the McCormick Reaper gained an edge. Farmers liked it. It did the job. McCormick's machines became popular in England and Europe, too. He added devices to tie the grain, as well as other improvements. McCormick's cutting principle proved to be the best in wet or dry conditions. Although his machines were more elaborate and more expensive, they could be pulled all day by two horses.

Still, farmers watched in wonder as the battle between reaper manufacturers continued. At one point, rivals McCormick and Hussey were hooking their reapers *together.* Then the teams of horses would be driven to their limit. The point was to see which machine could actually *tear apart* the other. Foolish? Perhaps, but the point was made to potential customers who wanted *strong* farm machines as well as efficient

ones. America was an agricultural country. These competitions were as important as auto races are today.

A gangling young lawyer from Illinois became involved in the reaper wars, too. In 1856, farmer John H. Manny decided to build a reaper similar to the one being marketed by Cyrus McCormick. *Very* similar. So McCormick sued Manny. It was an important case.

If Manny and his backwoods lawyer won, he could continue to manufacture his reaper. If McCormick won, he would almost totally control modern reaper design. He could collect royalties from almost every other reaper builder.

It was also the biggest case to date for the young Illinois lawyer. His fee, staggering at the time, was $500 in advance and $1000 payable at the end of the case. He used part of the fee to further his political ambitions with a race for a Senate seat (which he lost). He used part of the fee to build a home in Springfield, Illinois. That home is now a National Landmark.

The court held that John Manny had *not* infringed on McCormick's patents, and the young lawyer won the case. It was his first touch of fame, a fame that would eventually lead to the White House, for the lawyer's name was Abraham Lincoln.

McCormick wasn't really hurt by the case. He

Deere and Company was the largest manufacturer of tillage equipment and also wagons, carriages and even bicycles at the close of the 19th century. Deere also manufactured this popular "light running" grain binder from 1910 to as late as 1945. *(John Deere photo)*

continued to build and sell the most popular reaper, and in 1902 the McCormick holdings were merged with the giant International Harvester Company.

3

Threshers

REAPER BUILDERS, men who built machines to *cut* the grain, continued to slug it out. At about the same time, *thresher* builders were busy. A thresher is a machine that does four different things to grain. It removes the grain from the cob or husk, separates the two, cleans the grain, then gathers or stacks it.

The word "thresh," which was "thrash" in earlier days, suggests beating. In ancient times men used animals to trample grain and separate the seed from the pod. Sometimes they dragged rough or studded platforms over the grain to separate it. In fact, the "threshing sledge" is probably the oldest farm implement in recorded history.

The Old Testament prophet, Isaiah, wrote of threshing sledges in 720 B.C. And as recently as 1960

there were still more than *two million* threshing sledges in use on farms in the Middle East and Europe. The farmer brings his crop to the threshing floor. Then he spreads it in a circle up to a foot deep and forty feet in diameter. The heavy sledge is hitched to cows or horses and driven around and around over the crop.

Meanwhile, the farmer is stirring the crop until all of the grain has been separated and the straw has been finely chopped up. Then the grain is separated from the straw by "winnowing." The grain mixed with chopped straw is tossed into the wind. The grain falls back to the ground and the chaff is blown away.

Before combines became the most popular reaping and threshing combination, great threshers like this one were very popular around 1930. Grain was brought to the threshing site in wagons and threshed by the machine. Straw was blown out of the tube at the left. *(John Deere photo)*

The entire operation, which can take as long as two months and account for a crop loss of as much as thirty percent, is done today in some countries exactly as it was centuries ago.

Early-day threshers, real *machines* that separated the grain from the chaff, took many different forms. One had mechanical hooves and was developed by William Evers of Yorkshire, England, in 1768. William Winlaw's 1785 axial thresher was more like a meat grinder. It literally *ground* the grain from the husks. A man by the name of Wardrop invented a threshing machine in 1794 that attempted to imitate the action of human arms. It *flailed* at the grain to

separate it from the husk.

By 1830 threshing machines had spread throughout England and Scotland. H.P. Lee's machines were
popular, as were those of Andrew Meikle. These machines seemed to be doing the job better than many of
the others.

Farming had boomed during the Napoleonic
Wars, but after the Battle of Waterloo in 1815, which
ended the fighting, thousands of veterans returned to
their homes in England. Most of them were farm laborers, but there were no jobs for them. These men,
who would normally be threshing grain, had to watch
a new-fangled machine do the work of ten men. In
1830, bands of unemployed farm laborers roamed the

Five crewmen were needed to operate this great hillside combine in California in the early 1900's. There was the "mule skinner" (driver), the "leveler," the "header puncher," the "separator tender" or "combine man," and the "sack jigger" (sack sewer). *(John Deere photo)*

countryside burning threshing machines. In two years, they destroyed more than four hundred threshers. The machines were a symbol to the workers of their problems. Many of the rioters were arrested and brought to trial. Over four hundred of them were convicted and sent to prison colonies in Australia. Nineteen were executed. It was a difficult time in England.

Farmers stopped buying threshers. It made no sense to buy a machine that a mob was apt to destroy. So development of the thresher moved across the ocean to the United States.

At first, threshers were imported to the young nation from Scotland and England. Thomas Jefferson was a progressive farmer who imported one of the for-

eign machines. With it, he was able to thresh 120 bushels of grain per day. George Washington continued with the older methods, although he experimented with a new type of "threshing floor" on his farm.

By 1822, threshers were selling for around $325 to $375, depending on how much they would do. Most were from overseas. American inventors hadn't yet come up with a workable design. One super-deluxe imported model was called a "combined thresher" and sold for $500. According to a writer of the day, however, that was an "immense and unattainable sum for the ordinary farmer."

In 1840 there were more than seven hundred threshers on the market. Some were under United

Tractors became much more popular than horses or mules as "pulling machines" in the early 1900's. This Deere tractor is pulling a Deere combine.
(John Deere photo)

States patents, including one held by an American inventor, John Pope. Pope had been working to develop his thresher since 1802, and it was becoming fairly well known. Both foreign and domestic threshers became common sights in Virginia. They were introduced to Ohio in 1831, to Indiana in 1839, and to Illinois in 1847.

With the threshers came winnowing machines. Air was still used to separate the grain from the chaff, but farmers didn't merely throw the mixture up into the wind. Such methods could not keep up with the output of a threshing machine. So a *machine* tossed the mixture around in a blast of air.

In 1830, two itinerant threshermen named Hiram and John Pitts owned an imported thresher. The

brothers traveled from field to field, hiring themselves out with their machine to farmers who needed threshing done. When not working, they would experiment with their machine to improve it. Gradually they turned to manufacturing threshers. By 1852 they were producing the "Chicago Pitts" thresher, a fine machine that threshed 300 to 500 bushels per day. Other Americans were designing and building threshers, too. In fact, one writer of the day wrote that threshers were "being manufactured in every town of any consequence."

Nothing is wasted, even after the harvest. This "stalker" goes through and cuts and grinds the remaining corn stalks for animal food. *(John Deere photo)*

Joseph Hall was building a popular threshing machine. He built the "bull" thresher, so named because of the bellowing sound it made while operating. Joseph Wemple, a blacksmith, built still another thresher that gained some popularity. Then he sold out to Hiram Pitts and retired a wealthy man. Jerome Increase Case modified his own design into an improved model and went into production in 1844. The Case name is still popular in farm equipment.

The Pitts machine most nearly resembled threshers of later decades. It removed some of the seed from

Today, though, the boy shown can easily drive this mighty cotton combine and cover many times the area of the early-day harvesters. *(author photo)*

the straw by a rotating cylinder. This enabled more threshing to take place by a rubbing action as the grain moved faster through a small space next to the cylinder. Rows of metal teeth then combed the grain.

On more modern machines, the grain and straw pass through a separator, and a large screen lets the grain fall through. The straw is carried to a discharge port. Finally, a cleaning shoe removes the rest of the chaff by air pressure. The grain falls through sieves, and then onto scales for weighing. The remaining chaff is blown from the machine.

If only such a machine could also *cut* the grain. How that would speed up the harvest!

4

THE COMBINE

THERE IS A BRONZE PLAQUE on a boulder on a farm in Calhoun County, Michigan. The plaque is there to honor the man who invented the best workable *combination* between the reaper and the thresher. It was a machine which could cut the grain, then remove it from its shell or cob, and clean it. As you might guess, the huge machine was named a "combine."

The inventor, Hiram Moore, was many years ahead of his time with the combine he built in 1838. It was *decades* later before the combine became the important piece of equipment it is today.

Moore, with financial help from lawyer John Hascall and a Michigan senator by the name of Lucius Lyon, had a novel way of showing off his machine. He would start combining a wheat field on his farm early

in the morning. Spectators watched and marveled at the lumbering, noisy machine towed by twenty horses. The first wheat harvested would be rushed to Moore's own mill where it was ground and then hurried to the farmhouse kitchen.

There the flour was baked into biscuits and the guests would be invited to sit down to supper early that afternoon and enjoy food that had been still growing in the field that very morning.

Moore, who enjoyed wearing a black top hat in the field, became well known with his combine. He sent one of his machines to California in 1858, but not *across* the country. The huge combine was carried on a

An 1884 Shippee "Stockton Combined Harvester and Agricultural Works" combine in the San Joaquin Valley of California. Ninety of these 14-foot header machines were built, but a number of lawsuits resulted because they didn't seem to work too well. *(John Deere photo)*

ship around Cape Horn. During the California harvest of 1854, the combine harvested six hundred acres of wheat. Unfortunately, the machine set fire to a wheat field in 1856 due to an overheated bearing, and both the machine and the field were destroyed.

Although Moore's was the best combine of the day, it was not the first. Samuel Lane patented a combined reaper-thresher in 1828. Other "traveling thresher" patents (as the machines were then known) were issued to Ashmore and Peck in 1835 and to Briggs and Carpenter in 1836. Unfortunately, the patent office fire of 1836 destroyed records of these machines as well as many other priceless patent documents.

41

Still, it was Moore's machine that is considered to be the very first true *combine*. And it was Hascall's money, although it was a dream of Hascall's *wife* that started it all. Hascall had a twenty-thousand-acre farm and he wanted to grow wheat. But he knew that even with many workers he could not harvest that much wheat profitably. He told his family about his wish to grow wheat, and he described the problems.

Then one morning his wife told him about a dream she had had the night before. She saw in her dream a huge machine going over the prairie. It was drawn by horses, and it was *cutting* the wheat, then *threshing* it. She even told her husband how the ma-

An early day combine pulled by a team of thirteen farm horses and manned by three farmers. This was similar to Moore's combine first used in Michigan. *(International Harvester photo)*

chine looked and how it seemed to be working.

Hascall told Moore of the dream and that started Moore on the design. Eventually, with help from Hascall, Moore built the machine and it *worked*. The reaper and the thresher remained very important farm tools, since the combine did not come into general use until the 1900's. But the future was obvious.

Hiram Moore died in 1875 at the age of seventy-three. It was well over a half century later before a combine was used again on the same farms in Michigan.

California was one of the "breadbaskets" of the nation. Farmers in this far-west state could see the

logic of the Moore combine. In the thirty-year period from 1858 to 1888, over twenty combine manufacturing ventures were started in the Pacific region.

Some of these combines gained a measure of fame. The newspapers of the day reported that the Davis Brothers combine "took the crowds away from the bearded lady" when it was first displayed at the Oregon State Fair. Other combines became known in the west. There was Marvin and Thurston's model, and the combines of Young, Patterson, the Housers, Matteson and Williamson, Myers, Shippee, Best, and the Holts. Most of these machines were similar, each one developed by inventors or farmers who had a dream that they could build the best combine of all.

Farmers knew that the greatest costs of harvesting were labor and horses. Horses had to be fed and cared for, but without teams of them to pull the heavy combines, the job was impossible. So inventors began to experiment with steam power. Finally, in 1888, a farmer in California's Sacramento Valley put together a machine that did more things *first* than any other combine to that time. The man was George Stockton Berry and his steam combine was an amazing machine.

• Berry's combine was self-propelled. Not only would its great steam engine drive the reaper and thresher parts, but also the wheels, so that horses

Smaller combines work smaller fields. There is a machine for every application from one of the combine builders. *(International Harvester photo)*

were no longer needed.

• By burning the straw that might have been dropped behind, it got its power from its own waste.

• The huge machine could *plow* a field as well as harvest it. All the farmer had to do was hook a plow onto the rear.

• The header bar, or cutter, was *forty* feet across, the largest ever seen.

• For the first time in history, more than *one hundred acres* could be reaped and threshed in a single day.

• To top things off, Berry mounted lights on his combine so that it could work the fields after dark, the first time this had been done.

Berry wrote the following for *Farm Implement News*: "The machine I built this season for my own use . . . is as near perfection as a machine for that purpose can be made. The ground wheels are four feet tall and six feet in diameter. My header cuts a swath forty feet wide; it is made in two sections, and so arranged that it is handled with ease on very rough 'hog wallow' lands, at the same time making a clean cut wherever it goes. The separator is of sufficient capacity to handle all the grain that can be got to it. I have averaged this season about 92 acres per day. I cut in two days 230 acres. It does not take any more men than I used last year to handle it, and it does about twice the work."

Berry eventually built and sold four of his machines for $7000 each. They were used by big grain growers in the early 1900's. Berry himself was eventually elected to the California Senate to represent Inyo and Tulare Counties.

Harvesting costs using horse-drawn reapers and stationary threshers were about $3 per acre between 1890 and 1900. Prices for a crew with a self-propelled combine were between $1.50 and $1.75 per acre during the same years. The days of the reaper and thresher were drawing to a close.

Inventors have made many improvements in the farm combine since the early 1900's. Daniel Best built a fine self-propelled combine during those years. He would sell his machine, then move in with the farmer for a week to be sure the new owner understood how to use it. This was also the most successful time for the Holt brothers, who built another good combine. Eventually the Holts merged with Best to form a powerful combine company.

But even then, it was the vast Midwest and the western Plains where the greatest farmlands existed. Thousands and thousands of acres waited for massive crops of wheat, corn, and other grains. If a combine was truly needed, it was needed in the Midwest and the Plains states. The trouble was, there simply wasn't enough rain in some of these states.

Then farmers learned "dry farming" techniques and the last huge area for growing grain opened up. In dry farming, a field is used only every *other* year. The off year gives the ground time to absorb moisture for the next crop. So several-thousand-acre crops are grown every other year.

Combines became essential to the harvest of wheat on the great plains of the United States and Canada. Many of these huge machines thunder side by side in teams across the vast fields. In doing so they provide billions of bushels of wheat for our nation and

"Custom Cutters" such as these go from farm to farm along a harvest trail that stretches over 1500 miles and covers ten states. In 1981–82, cutters harvested more than two *billion* bushels of winter wheat. *(International Harvester photo)*

for many other countries throughout the world. Combines work the giant cornfields of the Midwest and other seed and grain land in other parts of the country.

Gradually the many smaller farm equipment companies grew together. Some merged or bought up

Modern combines in (*a*) corn, (*b*) wheat and (*c*) soybeans. (*a*—John Deere photo, *b*—Allis Chalmers photo, *c*—John Deere photo)

others. Today there are four giants and a few smaller companies. Massey-Harris/Massey-Ferguson is one of the largest. The others are International Harvester (from Cyrus McCormick's original reaper company), Deere and Company (including Best and Holt, among others), and Allis Chalmers Corporation. These are known as the "big four" in combine sales throughout the world. They sell more than ninety percent of all the combines in North America.

Combines are now built to work on hillsides, in smaller fields, on soggy, wet fields and under other

challenging conditions. Each company uses different features in its machines to try to attract buyers. Just like car or refrigerator manufacturers and other competitive businesses, each one feels that its combines are best. Generally, though, they all work about the same way.

A modern farmer can go to to work in this "office" in relative comfort, with dials and gauges and switches to control the great combine. *(Allis Chalmers photo)*

5

How The Combine Works

WHAT HAPPENS when a huge combine thunders through a field of wheat or corn, its turbo-diesel engine roaring? The farmer sits in relative comfort in an air-conditioned, sound-insulated cab with "negative" pressure. This means the pressure is slightly more *inside* the cab than *outside*. So there is always an *outflowing* of air, and dust can't get in.

The farmer might be listening to AM or FM radio with twin stereo speakers and Dolby sound. Or perhaps he or she is enjoying music from a tape deck. The farmer is in contact with the farmhouse by short-wave or CB radio.

Operating a combine is difficult, demanding work, but modern machines provide the farmer as much comfort as possible for the long days in the fields

54

during harvest time. He looks out at the crop and at the cutting bars through curved, floor-to-ceiling windshields and side windows. He sits in a comfortable padded chair, not the metal "bucket seat" of the old days. A console of buttons, switches, and gauges helps him steer and control the giant machine.

There are two popular combine systems working today. One has the threshing cylinder mounted transversely, *across* the machine. The other has the cylinder mounted *in-line*, or from front to rear. Each has certain advantages, but both work about the same way to thresh the grain after it has been cut.

Let's take a corn combine into a field ready for

Two views inside the cab of a modern combine. The farmer can perfectly control his giant machine with all the levers and dials. *(International Harvester photos)*

These are different types of cotton combines, called "cotton pickers" by farmers. *(John Deere photo)*

harvest. Corn stands tall with ears growing up and out from the stalk. The farmer wants the kernels of corn. That is his crop. Everything else is unimportant in this case.

One type of combine has the threshing cylinder mounted *across* the machine. This is a cutaway view showing the corn being cut and then carried to the threshing cylinder. From there the grain drops down through blasts of air from the fan and finally is carried up to the storage tank. The chaff is blown out the back end, as shown. *(courtesy Allis Chalmers)*

There was a time when a farmer would go into the field and remove the ears from the stalks by hand. Then he would thresh the corn from the ears by one of several hand methods. The job would be time-consum-

ing and grain-wasting. It would also be hot, difficult, dusty work.

Driving our combine into the field, we'll line up the *header* with the rows of the crop. There are several slots in the header and the rows of corn will slide into these slots. Low profile *dividers* skim along just above the ground, guiding even fallen corn stalks into the

The other popular type of combine has the threshing cylinder mounted in-line, like this one in a cutaway view. The operation is similar, with the cut crop being carried to the cylinder by moving belts and the grain being cleaned by a blast of air. *(courtesy International Harvester)*

gathering slots. The stalks are bent to the ground as the ears are removed. Then a turning *auger* screw carries the ears to a belt, and that carries them to the *threshing cylinder.*

As the ears proceed to the cylinder, they must pass over a door that drops open if a rock gets into the system. Rocks or large stones can do damage inside

the cylinder. In most modern combines, this rock ejection system is automatic.

While we are listening to pleasant music from a tape deck (or the latest farm reports on the radio) the corn moves into the threshing cylinder. No farmer can completely relax on a job as important as this. He must steer his combine along the rows perfectly. He must watch his gauges and dials. He must be sure his speed is correct. If he goes too fast, he will lose crop. If he goes too slow, he will lose time.

Into the cylinder go the ears of corn, many at the same time. The cylinder is turning and, by rubbing

This is a special combine for harvesting rice. It is mounted with tracks for work in extremely soft or muddy fields, but it still has a 190 hp engine and a 156-bushel storage tank, similar to dry land combines. *(International Harvester photo)*

and friction, grain is removed from the ears. The corn kernels drop through the screened cylinder where another auger carries them to *accelerator rolls*. Here the corn grains are moved through a high-speed blast of air to clean them. Then they go to another cleaner where air is blown through to finish the cleaning job.

Finally, the corn grains are lifted by an *elevator* to the *storage bin* on the combine. These bins will hold hundreds of bushels of clean grain, so the farmer doesn't have to stop and unload too often.

Meanwhile, the cobs and shuck and silk of the corn are passed out of the cylinder toward the back of

Here's a special combine for working on hillsides. The farmer remains level and comfortable in his cab while the header tilts to match the slope of the field. The combine is cutting wheat. *(Allis Chalmers photo)*

the combine. These remains fall in among the stalks that are left behind in the field as the combine moves forward. It is possible that the farmer will come back later to scoop up this material for animal food, or it may be left to rot and return nutrients to the ground when it is plowed under for the next crop.

When the storage bin on the combine is full of grain, the farmer dumps the load into a truck through an *unloading tube.* He can control this entire action, including moving the tube, from his seat in the cab. The entire bin can be dumped in only a couple of minutes.

A job that might have taken a farmer several days or even weeks is finished. His grain is clean and stored, and he can get on with other tasks.

In fact, this modern combine he is using might have interchangeable headers. The corn header can be removed and a wheat header, or a header for some other crop, put on instead. After dropping off the old header, the farmer merely drives the combine up to the new header and aligns with it. Then he drops in some attaching pins and connects the drive and hydraulic hoses. The job can be done in minutes and he can be off to another field.

Modern combines are very versatile farm machines. There are even combines with wide, fat tires or with treads for harvesting rice. Why special tires or treads? Because rice grows in extremely moist conditions, even under water. A normal combine might sink.

Many farmers and inventors worked on reapers and threshers, and then on "combining" the two. The result is a machine that has opened great fields to the cultivation of man's precious food.

By the late 1970's, the population of the world went beyond *four billion*. In many parts of the world farmers are still struggling with ancient tools and harvest methods. Many farmers in other countries have trouble feeding even their own families with the food from their farms. But American agriculture can meet the challenge, and nearly one fourth of the world's population is now being fed in some way by American farmers.

This is because of the marvelous farm combine, an invention that truly changed all or our lives for the better.

Index